The Night Is Always

Darkest...

A Young Man's Journey
On The Edge Of
Suicide

J. Michaels

First published by

Jason Schramm

October, 2006

Printed in the United States of America

Copyright © by Jason Schramm

ISBN

978-0-6151-3517-5

This book is dedicated to the brothers of a broken circle, on earth as it
will be in heaven

Ourpoet.com

J. Michaels

<u>The Night Is Always Darkest</u> is a collection of poetry originally written over a five-year period starting in 1994. The poetry was written in a series of notebooks that the author referred to as his *Bibles*.

J. Michaels turned eighteen years old on May 21st of 1994. Two years prior, a good friend from high school was shot and killed after a football game. On July 3rd, 1994 two of his dearest friends died in a terrible car accident. These friends were part of a circle of friends whom were so close they referred to each other as brothers and are referred to as such many times in the *Bible* poems. In February of 1996 another brother of the broken circle died in another tragic car accident. He was J.'s best friend. During this series of tragedies J. Michaels thought of his own death daily. Whether it was the manic depression that doctors diagnosed, or the desire to honor his friends and the pact they had made, or simply a normal teenage reaction to abnormal circumstances; he attempted on a number of occasions to end his own life. He drowned himself in drugs and alcohol, chose to shut down emotionally and socially except for partying constantly with his remaining friends. The one positive thing he did was to chronicle his pain and fascination with his own death through poetry. This book contains those poems in their entirety. He has chosen to publish these in hopes that they will give hope to other lost souls, for he has come through the other side of his battle in a strong and fantastic fashion. J. Michaels currently lives with his wife and two children, he has true happiness and contentment in his life, and he thanks God and his friends daily for the opportunity to grasp every new day. After reading the pages of pain, sorrow, disgust, love, and a tortured heart, keep in mind that his journey did not end with a fall into an abyss, but continues on, flying above the day to day in the world of the extraordinary.

<u>Full Moon Poem</u>

How beautiful the night is
How lovely is the day
The moon shall unite us
The sun will chase the evil away
Do not have fear
When the night comes
Nothing is there
That can stop the sun
Do not shy
From the sun's rays
Do not cry
Night will follow the days
Do not hide
From evil men
For inside
There is no truth in them
All that counts
Is true love
What's it about
What dreams are made of
As long as you dream
Night or day
When they scream
You won't hear what they say
As long as there are thoughts
In the back of your mind
You won't be at fault
If true love you can't find

Don't give up

Always try

For where there's hope

There's strength to cry

The night will hide

Our crying eyes

The sun is kind

Our eyes shall dry

I for one

Will not leave

Until night and day have done

What I believe

How beautiful the night is

How lovely is the day

The moon shall unite us

The sun will chase the evil away

J-Bird

The past 3 years we've spent as friends is truly
unforgettable.

The way we cried & the way we flied is definitely
untouchable.

We've been through the long & always remained strong even
when we were apart.

You're my bestest friend in the whole wide world & I love it
when you fart.

Together as one the day will come when we <u>all</u> sit in our
circle.

It will be neat & a feat to see them up in Bircle (a cool
place I made up).

It won't be long to sing a song & pull the almighty Grampa
Bong.

Love,

MOJO

<u>Ours</u>

Everything must be ours
A small thing here
A simple change there
Something to make it ours
Can't accept it as it is
We must change it
In some simple way
Tear a hole
Burn a corner
Anything to make it ours
Use it every day
Give it all our love
It will always remain special
Because it's ours
Some may call it destruction
We call it improvement
A little more comfortable
A little less normal
As long as it is ours
No matter what happens
Or what comes along
What we have made ours
Will always remain
Ours

<u>A Motto</u>

To Err Is Human

To Kill Is Destruction

To Live Is Futile

To Die Is Divine

<u>A Statement</u>

Up to Down

Right to Left

Front to Back

Side to Side

Love to Hate

Peace to War

Think to Thought

Life to Pain

Right to Wrong

Truth to Lie

Beginning to End

Time to Die

<u>Alcoholic Daze</u>

Love is true

For only you

From the bottom of this bottle

The world looks blue

Backyard

The sun shines

Caressing the changing leaves

The ghosts of many

Walk around me

It's seen so many

Come and go

Do you think

It knows

Where they've been

Sat and slept

Where we all

Hugged and wept

Does it miss them

As much as I

This is where

We learned to fly

Does it feel

The way I do

Spend its time

Missing you

I do

Free Spirit

As a child

I was so wild

Happy and carefree

As I grew

I took to you

And you took to me

Now you're gone

A sad song

Brings a tear to my eye

You're not around

But I have found

Your spirit in the sky

When in doubt

I find out

You are still with me

I wait for the day

The angels say

My spirit is set free

<u>I Love You</u>

Love is like a flower

All wilted and dead

What were those words

You once said

Love is like a flower

As the petals blow away

What were those words

You used to say

What were those words

That were so untrue

I remember the words

I love you

5/5/2000

Out comes the world

All green, blue, and white

Oh, what a beautiful site

Here on the dark side

All shades of grey

I despise every new day

The Earth is so beautiful

So innocent and pure

It hasn't been destroyed

By some stupid war

I bet there's enough oxygen

For people to breath

My father says

It's hard to believe

It must be beautiful, peaceful, serene

This place is so wicked, evil, and mean

I'll go there one day

Just wait and see

At least when I'm there

Everyone will love me

What are all those flashing lights?

The Earth has gone black as night!

Oh, well

Maybe the next one

Will be young

<u>The Hope of None</u>

8,000 miles

Down the river of dreams

I have traveled

And all I have seen

You would not believe

Green skies

And purple rain

Tell me you love me

You're all the same

I've seen life

Turn to death

And death's soft glow

I know things

You will never know

And in the end

When my trip is done

I will be

The only one

Standing alone

The dreams are gone

And all that remains

Is the hope of none

<u>Shine On</u>

Shine on

Like the waking dawn

Shine on

Cut through the night

With your beautiful light

Shine on

When the light dims

And begins, to fade away

Shine on

When gone is the light

With all of your might

Shine on

When, my friend

Comes the end

Shine on

And in death

As a baby's breath

Shine on

I will look for your light

When I enter the night

For me

Shine on

<u>Raining From Above</u>

A falling tear

Missed chance at love

Pain is here

Raining from above

Next shot at love

Given no chance

Raining from above

The devils dance

Deep pain inside

Missing the love

Can not hide

Raining from above

I've felt the pain

That follows love

Can't stop the rain

Raining from above

Perception

Silence can be

The loudest thing

In my ears

A single moment

Can last

A thousand years

The smallest pebble

Can be

A mountain range

The sanest man

Is sometimes

The most deranged

The deepest calm

Explodes in a

Violent rage

The great wide open

Becomes

An iron cage

A simple man

In truth

Is so complex

A soft virgin

Is truly

The meaning of sex

Death

Doesn't have to be

Sad

Life

Doesn't have to be

Bad

<u>My Friends</u>

We had what we had

It all went away

Waiting and waiting

For another day

The day has come

All my friends

All my friends

Are back again

Now the love

Fills the air

Whatever we want

Everything's there

All my friends

All my friends

We're back again

Am I dying?

Or did I die?

Not a person

Cared to cry

Perhaps we're back

Here to stay

Or are we just waiting

For another day

All my friends

All my friends

We're back again

Is this the end?

I know it isn't the beginning

Is this the end?

My friends

Powered by Love

A hole opens

In the sky above

A shining light

Powered by love

It's blinding me

With it's beautiful light

No more pain

I see only white

Just as a tear

Falls from above

The light surrounds me

Powered by love

It's time to go

They whisper gently

It'll be fine

Don't worry for me

I'm not alone

I'm with my friends

This is not a dream

This is the end

<u>Love is Gone</u>

The birds chirp

The day so pure

My disease

Has no cure

For I have loved

And I have lost

I have found

What it costs

If you give your heart

Completely in

Is that such a sin

I am paying

For what I have done

'cause I have loved

And the love is gone

<u>Good-bye</u>

The sun and moon

Walked by my side

From the truth

I can not hide

The time is up

And so is mine

The more I look

The less I find

The sun has set

It will not rise

The moon's gone down

Never to shine

I will go

With love in mind

And the end

I will find

Good-bye

Hold A New, New Angels Hand

You are so beautiful

This must be a dream

Nothing is this beautiful

It can't be as it seems

The first thing I think of

Is a lovely red rose

Almost completely closed

Who knows what it holds

Yet as each petal opens

My love grows ever strong

I find that on the inside

Is a beautiful waking dawn

And when our flower's open

The beauty has been shown

Our love for each other

Will be forever known

<u>Emotion</u>

Like a raindrop

Falls a tear

From the sky

Like blackness

Feel the sorrow

Say Good-bye

With death

Feel the pain

Ask why

With love

Feel the pain

Start to cry

When content

Try to relax

Heave a sigh

Feel the happiness

Give thanks

Start to fly

A Dream

A tear falling from my eye
A love filling my heart
Life without pain
A wife to call by name
A loving family
Above and below
Peace in my heart
Rest for my mind
A soul without a hole
A circle without a break
Happiness
Questions with answers
Problems with solutions
Love without loss
Life without pain
Birth without death
A friend that understands
Civilization without rules
A day without violence
Peace on Earth
Contentment of man
A mind without walls
A heart without blackness
A smile without a frown
A kiss without the past
Love without loss
Life without pain

<u>A Tear</u>

A tear falls from my eye
Death and destruction all around
Rain and tornadoes sweeping down
Trains, planes, and buses crash and burn
Blade in chest and turn
Earthquakes tear the Earth apart
In mother's hand is her child's beating heart
People chewing broken glass
Body parts left from the blast
A man stands with his testicles in hand
The color blood-red stains the land
Skinned carcasses of cats hung by their tails
A little late to save the whales
My mother said she loved me
My father didn't care
My brothers they all miss me
I'm the only one still here
A tear falls from my eye

<u>And My Journey Begins</u>

And my journey begins

I have no plan

No where to go

A lonely man

In a cold, cruel world

But I will find my way

I will remain strong

Maybe not today

But my time will come

I am meant for something

Something true and dear

And I will go to another place

If I can't find it here

And my journey begins

<u>Be Real</u>

I'm tired of walking tiptoe through life
Worried about who might get hurt
I'm tired of walking on eggshells
Too scared to kick up the dirt
I'm beginning to speak my mind now
God, does it feel good
If you don't like what I'm saying
Well, I never said you would
I'm done with playing for both teams
I refuse to be forced to pick sides
It's time to step out in the open
I'm tired of trying to hide
It's time to be outspoken
Tell everyone how I feel
It's time to stop pretending
It's time to finally be real

It's Time

I must go

For I know

It's time

I must leave

For I believe

It's time

I can not stay

There is no way

It's time

It is not right

To stay and fight

It's time

One last smoke

One more toke

It's time

I won't forget

The day we met

It's time

We'll meet again

Good-bye my friend

It's time

If I go to hell

Oh well

It's time

<u>Moon and Sun</u>

Here I fly

I am so high

Yet I am not scared

No breath escapes my lips

On this trip of trips

But still I have no fear

Here I fly with the sun

My trip is almost done

I do not fly alone

Hand in hand with the moon

The trip is ending soon

And then I shall be home

Gently I'm set down

Love is all around

I'm not the only one

Here I am again

Standing with my friends

I've flown with the moon and sun

The Boys Who Were Slain

A shot rings out
Of the cold black night
Fills my mind
With terror and fright
Did you hear the crash
The loud bang
Not a firecracker
Boys were slain
Feel the tightening
Of the noose
Just as your soul
Breaks loose
Feel the power
Of the train
One more boy
Has been slain
A car leaps out
A second of flight
Just before the driver
Says goodnight
No one left
To feel the pain
Of the boys
Who were slain

Searching

Spring has come

With all its splendor

A letter stamped

Return to sender

My search will continue

For all of my days

I search for you

A thousand ways

Will I find you

Will you come

I won't give up

'Til my time is done

On comes summer

With blistering heat

On I search

Until we meet

I can't forget

What we had

This love entraps me

I'm going mad

For one reason only

Do I continue

With hopes of one day

Finding you

<u>Remember</u>

What if I was to die?
Would it be so bad?
How long would you cry?
How long would you be sad?
Is a year enough?
Should you wait for two?
Until you can't remember?
Until the prophecies come true?
What's considered acceptable?
For how long should you care?
It really doesn't matter
I just won't be here
Remember our last kiss
Remember that I cared
Remember that I loved you
And this will always be
If I was to die
Would you die with me?
If I asked you to go with me
Is that how it should go?
Are there any answers?
I can never know
Remember our last kiss
Remember that I cared
Remember our last kiss
Remember that I cared

<u>Speaking to God</u>

You call this justice

This travesty of truths

Twenty years for evil

Life for good

You call this justice

This meaningless charade

Three of us had to die

For the mistakes we all made

You call this justice

The destruction of youth

You call this justice

Justice is not truth

You call this justice

You're living a lie

There'll be no justice

Until I die

On Another Day

A question in a question
Circles spinning 'round
Death and life are equals
When the wine comes pouring out
Alcohol's my best friend
The drugs can ease my mind
But they don't last forever
Even though they are so kind
My brain is exploding
Expanding inside my skull
My thoughts are not processing
Once again I've hit a wall
Talking doesn't help it
Crying's failing too
The wall of pain I've hit
Has left me no more to do
My heart has pounded
With love of all kinds
I've been severely wounded
As my time slowly winds
Now I'm waiting
That I shall stay
'Til death comes calling
On another day

No Fear

I used to dream my life away
But now those times are gone
All my dreams have run from me
Now I'm left with one
I dream of the day that I shall die
My pain will be set free
Many people try and try
But they could not help me
We can not hold all of our dreams
No matter how we try
But when we lose everyone
Then it's time to die
I don't want your pity
I'm not asking for your love
The only ones to help me
Are my brothers up above
Please my brothers take me
Don't make me suffer here
When death comes to embrace me
I shall have no fear

Love is a Crime

Must break free

From his grasp

You and I

Could never last

Run away

From his stare

I can not stay

There's nothing here

I must go

Before I'm caught

Love is pain you know

That's what I've been taught

My teacher is black

An evil man

He teaches fact

As only pain can

I must go

There's no more time

Pain is all I know

Love is a crime

<u>Give and Take</u>

Cry on my shoulder

Hold my hand

Let me be there for you

All I do is give, give, give

How can my life be true

It's time to learn

How to take

And keep what I receive

It's time to change this crazy life

To something I believe

Can I cry on your shoulder

Can I hold your hand

Will you be there for me

All I do is take, take, take

How can this life be

I must learn

Give and take

And equal out the two

And in the end

We shall stand

Simply me and you

<u>Echoes</u>

The ashes cold and gray
I watch them blow away
Floating on the breeze
Much like all the pain
They're all that does remain
Of a thousand trees
Once they burned so bright
In the darkness of the night
But now they all have gone
They stood so tall and proud
Touching every cloud
But now there is just one
It stands alone and cold
It looks so very old
Falling towards the ground
The memories they fade
Of where the trees once laid
Just echoes of the sound

A Fly's Life

Two short weeks with what to live
Buzzing from place to place
Forever to roam without a home
Stop and eat, whatever is sweet
Fly away, only to return
There's no need to learn
People swatting, becoming annoyed
They don't mind whose meal they've spoiled
Oh what a feast people love the least
Swallowing down a nice taste of shit
Try to remember to avoid the web
For if you don't you're dead
A rolled up magazine, you better fly away
If you hope to land another day
Sex in flight, what a sight
Breaking apart so suddenly
Leaving larvae in a garbage can
Little white maggots, disgusting man
A circle of life oh so short
To humans it seems so unimportant
As the fly swatter comes down with a splat
Goodbye Mr. Fly
You've died

A Time Once Upon

The children play

In their yards so green

Without a care in the world

Mothers sit

In their kitchens pink

An evil word unheard

A man slowly walks

Down streets serene

Stealing children's souls

The women remain seated

In quiet conversation

What's happened they don't know

Their children sit quietly

Staring blankly at the sky

Barely considered alive

Because of the man

The stealer of souls

A life they'll be deprived

The man

The devil's warrior

Walks freely on

To steal the souls of children

From behind their mother's eyes

A time once upon

<u>Anything</u>

Anything

Anything you ask with words or eyes

Anything you want

Anything you cry

Anything you need by blood, sweat, and tears

Anything you love

Any number of years

Anything you hate

All that you despise

You'll never have to wait

I'll see it in your eyes

Anything that's good

Anything that's pure

Anything that's late

Anytime you're sure

Anything that's sweet

Is yours

Anything I say

Anything I do

Anything I write

Is for you

Anything you love

Anything you need

Anything you want

Anything

Flight of the Dove

A glimmer of light
A shining hope
An end to this night
Impossible to cope
The light draws near
Continuing on
The end of fear
The light of sun
Reach of hand
Opened wide
Never a man
Has been inside
Tear through the night
With all rage
Break from the fright
An iron cage
Open the heart
Step inside
If torn apart
You tried
If access you gain
Filled with love
No more pain
Flight of the dove

<u>Mine</u>

I look

But I can not see

I listen

But I can not hear

I think

But I do not feel

What is wrong

With the love of some

I can not have

Everyone

What I have

Is none

For what I did have

Is gone

Waiting to Die

I've spent my time

Waiting to die

And my time is almost here

I know you'll miss

My soft kiss

But they have called me there

I looked away

Every day

They showed me I must go

I must respond

You'll carry on

That I'm sure I know

Do not cry

When I die

I died with them that night

Not a tear

Never fear

I'm reaching for the light

I love you all

As I walk this hall

Looking for the door to the end

Now I see

Your love for me

Thank you for being my friend

True Friends

I've done all I can
I've got nothing left
My heart lies here broken
Did I pass your test?
What more do you want?
How far must I go?
If I ask a hundred times
Will you still answer no?
I wish it could be different
Wouldn't have to be this way
But I can't change the world
Can't tell you what to say
So now I must go on
And forget there ever was
That place inside my heart
And the destruction that it does
I should have thought harder
I should have seen clear
But I chose to close my eyes
And see what wasn't there
Now once again I've learned
What is time and time again
That loneliness and sadness
Are my only two true friends

The Eye

Into the eye
A piercing stare
Must learn to fly
Find what's there
An empty hole
Consumes the heart
A lost soul
Torn apart
The missing link
The meaning of life
No time to think
It's time to die
A question why
Not a tear
Never cry
Never fear
Open the eye
Death is near
Begin to fly
The time is here

The Souls I Hold

You are the light
Inside my eyes
The love that fills
My heart
You're everything
I hoped for
But now it's time we part
I have learned
The secret of life
No longer do I belong
I will see you
All again
May the journey not be long
I've been told
By the souls I hold
It is now my time
I wish you well
With your private hell
Until it is your time
With love in heart
My journey starts
I'll think of you on the way
The time will come
We'll be as one
And we'll be together always

Standing At My Grave

Got a smoke?

I'm at the end of my rope

Can't you see I'm dying here?

I try to write

Too tired to fight

But do I really care?

Allow the pain

To fall like rain

And drench me with it's feel

I'm leaving now

Don't care how

This way is too unreal

I'm gonna cruise

To late to use

All to me you gave

In the morning dew

I'll find you

Standing at my grave

Summer Love

A summer breeze
Moving through the trees
Is there any better?
Under the sun's rays
On a bright summer day
That is where I met her.
Sitting on the bench
Surrounded by the sand
That's where we fell in love
Laughing in the shade
Hiding from the heat
Pouring from above
Lying under the stars
The whole world was ours
And nothing could stop us
The end of summer came
And with the fall came rain
That is when you left me
And when the summer comes
I think of what was
And lay flowers on your grave

No Surrender

I'm so completely tired
But I refuse to sleep
I will not give up
'Til I find out where it leads
If it takes me forever
Until the end of time
I shall continue
With every new rhyme
I must be going somewhere
Everything has an end
And this I believe
Can be my only friend
I can't put down my pen
Until it's finally done
A million meaningless words
Only to find one
My fight I will continue
I will never quit
As long as I'm still breathing
As long as I have whit
I will not surrender
I refuse to give in
You can try to stop me
But that would be a sin
I was put here for a purpose
And my purpose I shall find
As long as the words keep coming
And I can make them rhyme

Life's End

Give me a drink

I need to think

Sober's not the way

A straight flush

I may be a lush

But at least I can play

Roll a spliff

I need a lift

From this day to day

Pull a bong

Write a song

It's the only way

Take a dive

I'm still alive

But I will not stay

Cut a line

I'm feeling fine

Today is my last day

A falling tear

I'm going there

I must be on my way

Send a flower

With all my power

I just could not stay

<u>Gemini</u>

Punish me

For all my wrongs

Destroy my being

For all I've done

Send me to hell

It's where I belong

I deserve pain

For all I've caused

I do know

Right from wrong

Yet I've chose the latter

Should I beg

For you to forgive

When your heart I shattered

What comes around

Goes around

This is true I've found

As a Gemini

My evil twin

Has destroyed the other

Too late to cry

Too late to sigh

Too late to make it better

Now it's time

To fall behind

Before my heart grows sadder

Grim Happiness

I don't want to love anymore
I don't need the pain
But I can't turn my back
On those that do remain
Please just come and take me
Get me outta here
I've asked so many times
But you won't bring me there
The past has turned it's back on me
The future shall not come
My life is filled with hate
Got some pain? Gimme some
It's all that I can feed from
Gives me drive to stay alive
Show me a pool of burning fire
Then step away while I dive
Death is all around us
We see it every day
The day is soon in coming
The day we all shall pay
I will go out smiling
So happy I will be
When the Grim Reaper's bony finger
Outstretches to point at me

<u>Heavenly Dreamin'</u>

I've seen what is to come

After I die

All my friends that in the past

Said goodbye

Sitting and talking

Together again

Laughing and smiling

My friends

All looking

The best we've ever looked

Once again whole

No pages missing from our book

Those we left behind

They get the point

The words and love we left for them

Will make them join

I never could have imagined

How it would be

Now that I have been there

As if the blind could see

It doesn't really matter

Of the land

The love of all my loved ones

Returned to my hand

Dance With the Devil

Day in, day out

A silent shout

Is anyone there

Does anyone care

This is untrue

You know that they care

Everyone cares

But you

Why don't you die

Go ahead cry

At this rate

You'll never fly

End it all

This is last call

If you fail

The ship will sail

Leaving you behind

Be a man

I know you can

Come on die

I'll teach you how to fly

Come let's dance

You haven't a chance

You're mine

Fine

<u>Easter Afternoon</u>

Back again

An Easter afternoon

The day of reckoning

Coming soon

I walk

Slowly

Thinking of

The way it used to be

Swallowing

Has become

The hardest thing to do

Writing

My life

For me

I know

I see

Do you?

You can't

I must

I'm free

Dying

From the inside

Out

Laughing

On the outside

As I shout

I pray

My day

Coming soon

My love
I hope
I go with you

A Bible's End

Another Bible
Has come to an end
Dedicated to Joey
My best friend
I love you my friend
Always did
Friends 'til the end
We never hid
I told you everything
You understood
If you couldn't
I knew you would
To look into your eyes again
To see inside your soul
The place you had inside of me
Has now become a hole
But it will be filled
When we meet again
It will come soon
I'll see you my friend
I've loved you always
I always will
You loved me also
You love me still
I can't wait to meet you
On the other side
When we're back together
I won't need to hide

I will wait
'Til I go too
I pray to God
That it will be soon

A Question?

I've got a question
One that's never been asked
I've got a question
One that can not be passed
I've got a question
Burning a hole in my heart
I've got a question
I just don't know how to start
I've got a question
A question from deep in my soul
I've got a question
Something that no one can know
I've got a question
It could change all of mankind
I've got a question
To withstand the test of time
I've got a question
Perhaps I shouldn't say
I've got a question
I'm asking it today
I've got a question
A question that will lay
I've got a question
I'm afraid there is no way
I've got a question
A question I will keep
I've got a question
That will forever sleep

I've got a question
There's no need for you to pray
I've got a question
A question it will stay

All I Do

All I do is smoke now
I need a drink
To think
All I do is sleep now
I need pain
To remain
All I do is cry now
I need sorrow
For me to grow
All I do is smile now
I need blow
To let me go
All I do is fly now
I need death
To catch my breath
All I do is eat now
I need meat
To reach my feet
All I do is write now
I need words
To save my world
All I do is live now
I need time
To pay my crime
All I do is love now
I need you
To make it true
All I do is nothing now
And that is all I need

<u>All We Are</u>

How long can I keep up
This meaningless charade
For I truly do not love you
A mistake is what I made
This may not be fair to you
My decision may be wrong
But I could never love you
And I've known this all along
So why did I do it
A question you may ask
Because I thought I gave a shit
I thought that it might last
I forgot I care for nothing
I felt that I should care
If you should ask for loving
There can't be any there
I'm sorry for lying to you
I'm sorry for what I've done
But I can't change what's true
I can't be the one
Now this lie must end
Before it goes too far
I'm truly sorry my friend
For that is all we are

Chow Bella, Sainta Jude

I can't remember

The way you looked

The life inside your eyes

Now when I think of you

I look up to the skies

A kiss for peace

Held to my heart

To show I'm thinking of you

Without your love, I am lost

I don't know what to do

I bow my head

I start to cry

The sadness that I feel

To think that I

Can endure this pain

The idea's too unreal

I'll never forget

The way I felt

When we were so close

All I can do

Is have a drink

And send a little toast

Chow Bella

Sainta Jude

<u>For My Valentine</u>

Sweets for my sweet
Love for my love
My heart goes to you
Which you destroyed
All the love I've seen
All the love I've made
All was just a farce
A tree that lends no shade
All the pain I've felt
All the love I feel
It doesn't matter anyway
None of it is real
All my future hopes
All my future dreams
Everyone has a mate
Life isn't as it seems
Everything I give
All that I do take
Living life for love
Fighting for truth is fake
No point in what I want
No point in what I have
All that I search for
All isn't even half
What the hell is love?
Explain to me pure joy
In the body of a man
I will always be a boy

I Will Write

I'm not really sure
Why I bother to write
It's yet to take me away
It seems a bothersome
Waste of time
Yet I do it anyway
A tedious task?
No, not really
But it doesn't really help
It may help another
Who reads it one day
That's how I once felt
I lack the wisdom
I'm short on years
And I do not want them to come
I'm full of sorrow
Full of tears
But those can't help anyone
I feel it's useless
There is no point
I feel I should just quit
I've done it so long
I've written my heart
No one gives a shit.

What Life Is All About

How can I know
What I feel?
The damage that's been done
How can I believe
That this is real?
When you and I were one
How can I cry
When I think of you?
If I don't think you've gone
How can I smile
And speak of you?
When I'll never see you again
What am I
Supposed to do?
It's hard to say your name
We spent our time
Waiting for the end
For you it finally came
The love I feel
The tears that fall
All they add is pain
What we had
Who we were
Driving me insane
If I could find you
In my heart
I'd have to tear it out
All the blackness
All the pain
What life is all about

The Cheesy Way Out

The door to the future, lies in our past
The love's been forgotten, nothing ever lasts
A tear fills my eye, my gentle whisper dies
A man's not a man, if that man never cries
A gentle breeze, a deadly hurricane
My love for you is strong, driving me insane
The rain is pelting, soaking my clothes
My heart is breaking, and no one knows
I can't leave who I was , behind me
I can't be who I am, without he
I long to live my life, for you
The first time I don't know what I should do

I'm dying

I'm crying

I'm sighing

I'm trying

Are you?

Special

Are we truly special?

What is meant to be?

I'm not saying we are better

But will I ever see?

We've always felt so special

So different in our ways

Are we like the others?

Simply counting down the days

I can not believe

That everyone's the same

I've always felt so different

And that feeling will remain

We'll always think we're special

The difference that will be

For if you think you're normal

That's all you'll ever be

I still believe I'm special

No matter what you say

And this I shall believe

Until my dying day

You may say that I'm conceited

But this simply isn't true

I only said that I am special

Not any better than you

And if you think I'm wrong

You're opinion you may have

But I'll still think I'm special

And that will keep me on my path

Only A Glance

Turning backs to the past
The open road staring up
Looming ominously ahead
The mountains of the west
Possibilities are endless
Loose ends are left untied
Hair floats on the wind
A smile spells out goodbye
Nothing but a tear
Falling to the ground
What is done is done
Useless to look around
A promise escapes her lips
A promise that will not come
Happiness is deserved by most
Love is only for some
Word arrives years later
Of the day that she'll be wed
A vision crosses his mind
Her in another's bed
More beautiful than ever
The day that she is wed
He watches through the window
Much to say, nothing said
As she jumps into the limo
She thinks she caught a glance
Of the man that she once loved
Wishing for another chance

<u>Nothing Lasts</u>

It's strange how fast things can change
Within a single blink of an eye
Those who wanted you dead
Are now in love with your smile
False accusations
Sparked by insecurity
One second you feel so clean
The next you feel so dirty
It's weird how things can happen
The smallest thing changes your mind
Someone that made you sick
Can make you want to be kind
Things can change so fast
It happens as you watch
Everything is different now
Reality is now a crock
People's feelings sway
Quickly to and fro
It raises silent questions
What really do you know?
Things can change so fast
Nothing you'd expect
Now has become the truth
Built upon the wreck
No need to feel guilty
You did nothing wrong
Everything must change
Nothing lasts that long

<u>Look</u>

Look at the world
Through different colored eyes
It's good to have a change
Once in a while
Imagine the world
As if this was the norm
Imagine if the sky was green
And the snow that fell was warm
If the sun's bright rays
Threw darkness on the land
And if a world of peace
Was the final downfall of man
Imagine if love was always true
And would forever last
Imagine if no one ever died
Nothing faded in the past
But in imagination
Is all that this may be
Perhaps the key to happiness
Is the way we look at things

A New Year

As the New Year unfolds, before our very eyes
Our love has been confusing, filled with crying eyes
Your pain is so exceeding, mine along with yours
For the loves of our lives, both our hearts do burn
Yours is for my best friend, mine burns on for you
We hold onto each other, it's all that we can do
I will not try to stop you, when your path veers off away
I love you with all my heart, good enough for today
Perhaps you're blinded by sadness, and together we can't see
What lies ahead in our future, love for you and me
As one forever, we've always been so close
Until our times here end, understanding more than most
Partners in pain, sorrow, love, and tears
Together until, the end of our years
It may not be so, the love may not grow
And always we'll be best friends
If I love you as much as I do, you as much as you can
We'll be together as one, until the end
Whether in love or as best friends
Matters not to me
In my heart you'll be so special
Always so special to me
We start this year together, together we may end
But if our love should falter, we'll always be best friends

<u>A Prayer to Forgive</u>

I never knew love

Until I found it

With you

I don't know

How I'll live

Without you

I must go on

Even though

I want to stay

For I've lost your trust

And with it your love

Never to regain

I took the most beautiful thing

I've ever known

And threw it away

After I did it

I didn't know

What to say

I wanted to hold you

And tell you

It'll be okay

The only thing left

For me to do

Is pray

Another Day

She tells me she loves me
She needs time to think
Maybe she doesn't mean it
My heart begins to sink
I tell her I love her
I believe it is true
Can it ever be?
Can the problems be worked through?
Her hearts being pulled
Two separate ways
Will it be torn?
Should I be on my way?
Could I stay?
Would it be right?
Is it my place?
Is it my fight?
Should she be left?
Alone with her thoughts
In her decision
Will a lesson be taught?
Thoughts of the past
Faded memories
It's been so long
I've loved her always
She was never mine
Perhaps she'll never be
I will still love her
When she doesn't love me

Goodbye my love
Is all I can say
We'll meet again
Another day

<u>Circles</u>

Life just runs in circles
Stumbling over itself
A clumsy young animal
A perfectly fine tuned machine
What comes around goes around
This I've found is true
And in the opposite direction
It leads to me and you
Life is little circles
All spinning on their own
Inside one big circle
Everything spins around
Life is infinitely tiny
Yet huge at the same time
And we are just one part
Continuing to go around
Some people think of a beginning
Some people think of an end
But in reality
Life truly does go on
All of these circles
Going round and round
Life is truly evil
And gentle I have found

<u>Fire</u>

Look into the fire
Feel it's intense heat
Don't choke upon the smoke
Breath it in deep
The fire can not hurt you
Unless you allow it to
The fire won't attack you
Unless you show it fear
The fire will respect you
If respect you show in turn
For if you truly love it
You shall not be burned
Fire is alive
It eats, it thinks, it breaths
You must accept it's beauty
It's no different than you and me
Never try to control it
Simply watch, and care, and feed
It will dance with you
And give you what you need
It will give you all of it's warmth
And help to light the way
It can turn the black of night
Into the brightest day
It's true I do love fire
Down to the last glowing speck
And it returns my love
For I show it respect

<u>If I Died Tonight</u>

The music's stopped
I don't know why
I feel as if
I'm about to die
It's been two years
Since our first broke through
Two long years
Without those two
And as we healed
Gathered in strength
Close to where we were
In the early days
Another left
To make the trip
The strongest link
They had to rip
Once again
We're trying to heal
Nothing's the same
It doesn't seem real
We play along
Like we'll be alright
Yet I wouldn't mind
If I died tonight

Mother Nature

Is technology the savior
Or shall it bring the end?
Messing with Mother Nature
Our only true friend
No one stops to think
What the consequences may be
Progress only pushes forward
Destroying all the trees
A world of concrete and silver
Is this where it shall lead?
How long can Mother Nature
Continue to bleed?
I can not see the future
For me it can't exist
The end of Mother Nature
Will she even be missed?
What the Hell are we thinking?
Destroying all we have
Pushing ever forward
No matter what is in our path
My views, you can not change them
For I will always believe
You can mess with Mother Nature
But she'll refuse to leave
Because of that she'll kill us
Each and every one
And she shall start all over
With a newborn glowing sun

V

A five year old man

In a nineteen year old body

Isn't that what you said

I'm so young

So immature

I need my pain spoon-fed

If I'm five

Am I alive?

It's what you said

Should I be dead?

A child's mind

Trapped inside

Screaming for relief

Cruel little twists

Acid flashbacks

I'm filled with false beliefs

If I'm five

Am I alive?

It's what you said

Should I be dead?

Under the eclipse

Moon over Sun

The child's time has come

Over the eclipse

Sun over Moon

The man has come too soon

If I'm five

Am I alive?

It's what you said

Should I be dead?

Two Sides to Every Coin

Black and white

Dark as night

Light of day

The sun shall play

Float upon a pink glowing cloud

As the sun sinks in the west

Fall faster, harder to the ground

Lie broken with the rest

Sing your song

Shout with pride

Find a place

It's safe to hide

Climb the mountain

Reach the top

Fall deeper in depression

When will it stop?

Cruise to the moon

Dance with the stars

Take my love

Crush what was ours

Pass the pyramid

On your way to hell

Life is good

Live it well

The Looking Glass

Are you all a bunch of fucking loons?

Do you realize what you are?

Is your point in life to make me sick?

Well you've pushed me too damn far

Why can't you just be real?

Why must you play this game?

Is it too hard just to fuck it?

Are we all the same?

Am I exactly like you?

If I turned my eyes around?

Would I be able to stand it?

Or would I tear it down?

Should we dare to test it?

Come let's give it a try

And if I don't come back

Remember not to cry

I looked a little too closely

There was so much there to see

And I have found a stranger

The stranger that is me

<u>Jerry Garcia Aug 9, 1995</u>

To count the lives

That you have touched

Would be anything but easy

The list would never end

You were our true friend

A father to so many

The words you wrote and sang

They shall always remain

We will not forget

I'll never forget the day

I first heard you play

And in my mind we met

I you never knew

But I still loved you

And that is the true test

Now that you are gone

We listen to your songs

You truly were the best

Thank you for living

Thank you for giving

Thank you for being our friend

But as the saying goes

And too well we all do know

All good things must end

Good-bye Jerry

<u>A Picture</u>

A moment in time

Caught suspended

A phantom of feelings

A ghost of the past

Trapped forever

Behind a piece of glass

A gentle smile

A silly smirk

A funny face

Not meant to last

Only a millisecond

Gone that fast

Now it's saved forever

Every little thing

A smudge on the mirror

A ball of lint on the couch

The load of worries

In the slightest slouch

A piece of the past

Pushed to the present

What was written

Is only read

What was alive

Is now dead

Father Death

Dreams unlock the secrets
Can show the other side
All the silly scientists
Can search the universe-wide
They can find nothing
That could possibly compare
To the love and the beauty
That I have seen there
In good spirits
I can say
I do not fear death
If it comes calling today
For I have seen
What is to come
Not just for me
But for everyone
So men, women, and children alike
Bow your head and thank Father Death
For he's come to take you there

<u>It's Coming</u>

Look into my eyes

That's death

I'm just waiting for it to come

It's coming

The winter

Death

It's coming

Coming to me

Like a soft kiss

A gentle breeze

The sound of the crickets

And the smell of summer

It's coming

And I love it

<u>Maybe Then</u>

Do I disgust you?

Do I make you sick?

If I don't, I should

My life

If you want to call it that

Is a joke

At one time I was filled with love

I think

I gave it to my brothers

The girl of my dreams

All are dead or dying

If only by my hand

I knew I couldn't be happy

I knew it could never be

But I still chose to chase it

Oh so foolishly

Put a knife in my hand

I'll plunge it into my chest

Put a gun to my head

I will do the rest

Rip my arms and legs off

Things I no longer need

For I will never hold again

No point for me to leave

I'm going to push everything away

Live my life alone

Until I die someday

Maybe then I will be home

Who Knew?

I had my hands
On the teachers edition
Of the Book of Life
But I traded it away
For a picture
Of tomorrow
The picture I gave
To a man standing
At his own grave
In return
He gave me
A chance to learn
I sold that chance
For the cash
To buy the world
I used that cash
To buy
A single bird
The bird flew away
Leaving behind
Only a feather
Perhaps tomorrow
My day
Will turn out better

<u>True Sun</u>

A hill

A golden sunset

Rising

Eastward

A line

The line between night and day

You see it?

I know

Starlight forever shining

A milky moon lies to rest

Cottony clouds

Pillars of smoke

Flames licking in a secret dance

Sun burning

Green grass and trees of old

Newfound life on every branch

Gentle breeze blowing

Whispering your name

Love

Love

Love

Sounds nice doesn't it?

The Door

A swinging door

That can only open

But one way

As it swings

We see quick shots

Of the other side

To push the door

Is to commit

The greatest crime

Not to look

But to ignore

Is to close your eyes

A swinging door

The reward

Of all time

The end

The peace

So kind

The door

That swings

To and fro

The exit

And entrance

For these that had to go

I will wait

Oh so patiently

Until the door

Swings wide

Opening for me

The Sword

The pen is mightier
Than the sword?
The pen can only
Bring the word
The sword can end
All the world
The pen can bring out
Peace
The sword can bring out
Death
Death is mightier than the rest
Ask yourself
What truly do you fear
Your fears are true
For death is near
You can write a letter
To say goodbye
But when the sword falls
You still shall die
The pen can bring out
People's hearts
The sword can take those hearts
And tear them out
The pen is mightier
Than the sword?
The sword will have
The final word

<u>Soul of a Child</u>

Want to see me cry?

Tell me you love me

That's all I need

As I watch you die before my eyes

If you don't I will

If neither of us do

We'll fall apart

Trust me I know

It's just a matter of time

I can't have love

It makes me laugh

I can't have love

I can only have pain

Hate

Destruction

Sorrow

Not love

Anything but love

I once knew what love was

Once

Until it was taken from me

Torn from my grasp

My heart is a stone

My tears ice

My blood doesn't flow

I'm a machine with the soul of a child

Grace

I wish I could close my eyes

Sleep the deepest sleep

Never to awaken

No more pain

I have nothing left

Yet things are still being taken from me

In death

In life

Only I can quench the thirst of the beast

My blood

My flesh

That's what he wants

Oh it tastes so sweet

I want to give it to him

I want him to take me

But he wants me piece by piece

Savoring the meal

Chewing each bite a thousand times

Then slowly biting off another piece

I am his meal

My blood is his wine

My flesh his meat

My mind remains intact

My heart is his dessert

This devil slowly chews

While I lie here in agony

It will be so many years

Before I'm finally set free

<u>Empty Promises</u>

A man past his prime in life kneels beside a grave with his head softly
drooping and his eyes slightly closed

His features are barely distinguishable against the dark backdrop of the
impending night

He remembers how many times he has stood next to a grave to grieve the
loss of yet another loved one

There is something that makes this time vastly different from all the
other times

Perhaps it's the sweet smell of a promise, summer, hanging in the air
Reminding him of the promise he made oh so many years ago

"I love you and I'll love you always, I'll return one day, you'll see", aren't
those the words he used?

He did not lie, but rather waited too long. He lost her love to another

He was never a man to blame, himself or others, but now that he has lost
the only person he ever loved, the sadness of life swallows him once
again

Memories of her smile, her laugh, her tears as they rolled down her
cheek, her eyes that could look through him straight into his soul.

She gave to him a love that no other person ever could. A love that was
true

Now that she is gone, what was left of him has died too.

<u>Child Eyes</u>

The single most amazing thing I've found

The gentle softness, innocence of a baby's eyes

Looking upon each thing with a sense of fascination

Fascination of setting their eyes on something for the first time

A feeling of excitement, inquisitiveness, adventure

There is no fear inside of them, no sense of regret

They don't know sorrow or pain

All they know is to find the beauty in all they see

A child's eyes do not see hate, it must be taught

They do not see in ignorance, only inexperience

To look into a child's eyes is a true test

For a man will see a reflection of himself

Not a mirror reflection, a reflection of his soul

No one can hide from a child's eyes

They see right through us into the depths of themselves

They search for only one thing, simply enough, beauty

Beauty of any kind, not marred by the hate and ignorance

Those things that have been instilled in us our entire lives

They look for the smallest piece of beauty inside

Yes, I'd have to say the most amazing things are a child's eyes

Try your best to use them

Look at the world through child eyes

Always try to find the beauty hidden there

<u>I'll Give</u>

I'll put fear in the hearts of the brave
I'll put strength in the souls of the weak
I'll cause doubt in the minds of the sure
I'll give death to the hands of a child
I'll give depth to those who are shallow
I'll give life to those who have died
I'll give peace to those at war
I'll give fears to those with joy
I'll give hate to those with love
I'll give happiness to those who have none
I'll give friendship to those who have not
I'll give soul to the men in suits
I'll give spirit to those in the street
I'll give blood to the ones in need
I'll give flesh to the flame in you
I'll give myself for any dream
I'll give my life for the smallest thing
I'll give my mind for a little love
My heart for some pain
My pain for you
What I can not give
My dream must stay true

<u>It's True</u>

Are you ready?

Ready to live alone

It's been a long time

Do you remember how?

Don't worry

You'll never truly be alone

You have love

You have friends

You always will

She won't leave you

Forget about you

She loves you

It's true

You'll be strong

Get along

Make it on your own

You'll be together again

And then

You'll know

This love

To you

Will never die

It's true

<u>My Pain</u>

One

Two

Three

And more

Come let's go for four

I've lost myself

In life and death

Look into my eyes

The windows to my soul

What was my soul

Now you can only see pain

A pain more intense

More intense than anything you could ever know

Let me give you my pain

Just for a moment

Your whole life will change

You'll never be the same

It will consume you slowly

Chewing, ripping, tearing, swallowing

One small chunk at a time

I have nowhere to go

Nothing to stay for

Floating, suspended

Timeless

Dying

Crying all the way

Let me give you my pain

Just for a moment

Then I'll take it back again

Winter Wind

The wind blows
Lifting the soft grains of snow
Changing them
They are now
Cold, bitter shards of ice
Biting into the trees and houses
Brutally whipping
The faces of children
Cruelly killing
The men of the street
No longer a soft blanket
Gently coating the land
A thousand bullets
From a never-ending arsenal of guns
A cold war
Slowly tearing away
At the heart of man
Ripping, crushing, chewing
Relentless destruction
Followed by peace
As the flakes of snow
Float gently to the ground
Once again

The Beasts

I stand alone
Amongst the flaming pillars of Hell
The demon beasts crowd around
With fire in their eyes they look hungrily at my flesh
The dark secrets that they hold
Slowly shown to me as they devour my meat
I have not died
I'm still alive
Strangely I feel no more pain
The sorrow has left me
I've realized my purpose here
To be an evil man
I feel comfortable with Satan's beasts
Finally someone loves me
Unconditionally
I will walk amongst the beasts
Revel in their strength and glory
I will crush those who stand in my way
Those I've loved in the past
Those who refused to love me
Stand back, turn away, you've all done it before
It's the only way to save yourselves
For I will never die

Starting Again, Again

The words come slowly
But at least they come
It's been so long
I never should have let it go this long
Still, the words do come
That's so important to me
If I couldn't write
I don't know what I would do
I must try to write more
Now that I've started again
I have to try to keep it up
God gave me this gift
It would be wrong to waste it
I've wasted so much in this life
But my life is not over
I still have time to save myself
I pray that I can find the will to do it
I can't let myself be a waste too
I must keep going on
Perfection is widely sought after
But seldomly attained
My life can never be perfect
But I can still make it worthwhile.
Goodbye

Life

Finally I've learned to fly

Watching the ocean speed by below

It's blue and brown, so beautiful as I pass

Occasionally I slip beneath the cool surface

Only to rise and fly again

I come to places and faces I once knew

To them I throw a smile

There's no time to stop, I press on

This feeling of flight fills me with joy

Joy I have never known before

At times I slip too deep

I worry for I am running out of breath

Just as I think I won't make it

I break through the surface with a gasp

It now takes time to return to flight

But eventually somehow I do

With every new flight increases the joy

No one can fly forever

We all must slip at some times beneath the cool surface

If we fight to rise above the water

The flight will return with time

When I sink so deep

When there is no time to return

Then I shall begin to fly higher than ever before

Above the clouds with the beautiful doves

House of the Devil

The house lying dark and dismal
Soulless, heartless, dying in the night
Silent occupants scream no more
Voices harsh, a whisper barely audible
The stench of decomposing flesh
The strange, prickly feeling of death
Wood long ago rotten cracks and creaks
A torch almost too good for this Hell house
Children speak nursery rhymes of the old place
The house upon the hill
Look it lies there still
Behind the patch of fog
Waits the Devil and his dog
For those that do go near
Fill yourself with fear
The Devil waits for thee
You shall set him free
The children's rhyme in part speaks the truth
For this is where the Devil resides
The gates of Hell on top of that hill
Waiting for us all to die
Once you walk inside those doors
It's then too late to cry

<u>Don't Cry</u>

A light with brilliance stronger than the Sun

Days and nights pass

Death rears it's ugly head

Not one but two

Destroyed

A light with brilliance softer than the Sun

Nights and days pass

Death rears it's ugly head

One more gone

Demise

A light without the brilliance of a flame

Day and night no longer exist, only time

Death shows it's kind hand

I am gone

Despise

A light

No more time

Death decides to come again

To take the two that do remain

Delight

A light with brilliance stronger than the Sun

Time is all we have

Death is done

A circle again

Don't cry

<u>Endlessly</u>

I have embarked upon a new journey in my life

Although slow going at first, faith will speed it along

I have chosen a path to ultimately reach my love

Unfortunately this path called for me to leave my love

Forcing myself to release her in order to one day return

Easily one of the most difficult times of my life

I've tried to die and failed, carried brothers to their graves

None of these were easy, none did I enjoy

I deserve more in my life, I deserve her smile

I will fight until I find it, fight every day for her

For I know that she is worth it, this gentle love of mine

The day we join together, never to part again

I shall shed a tear, a single tear of joy

As strong as my heart aches for this day I must wait

For nothing is given, all must be earned

I must earn her love for me, although I give mine

She has earned my love, simply being her

My gentle love, I would live for her

Time spins our future, this can not be rushed

Quietly I'll wait, wait for our day to come

My love, I give, Endlessly

For you

After Life

The Sun beats down on the now dry dirt

Trees and foliage of the past are gone

Torrential rains flood the deserts

Those trapped inside their houses

Forced to watch as their bodies wither away

Those outside scavenge for food

Giant boils raise from their skin

The Sun a round yellow orb in a black sky

In the night the moon is only a memory

The only light is thrown by constant lightning bolts

And raging fires devouring all

Animals have all been killed for food

Now scavengers have turned to human flesh

Pre-cooked by the blazing Sun

Insects are the only living things in great numbers

With the plentiful food and strange thick air

They've grown to immense sizes

There were reports of a millipede the size of a train

Of course there's no way of telling facts from fallacies

There is only one fact true to everyone

Death is ever present and widespread

The reaper is busy sewing his crops

We can only wait for him to come

For him to make us free

Facing West

Shit, shave, and shower

I'm leaving you a flower

Chavez

What was

Guiseppe Pascual

We knew you'd fall

Ciao Bella, Sainta Jude

Happiness we pursued

Ruby Begonia

I wish I had told you

Security

You and me

Farce, Facade, Bamboozled, Fiasco

Why didn't we know

You were my best friend

Friends until the end

Together we laughed

Cried and sighed

I wish together

We could have died

You left me

With nothing

No one

Slowly I'm dying

Not fast enough

Should I come join you?

I think yes

Where will I find you?

Facing west

I Cry

My life thus far has been a joke
A cruel joke played by cruel minds
Do you know what it is to be alone?
Sometimes I feel that's all I know
I've never found a love that didn't leave
Day by day, I feel myself slowly dying
Self pity
I deserve it
Do you know what it's like to be happy?
If you do, please tell me, I'd like to know
They ask me to go on
To stay here for them
But no one will stay for me
I only ask for one simple thing
I ask that they please
Just love me
But this is too much to ask
I can love, it's what I have to do
But no one can love me
Sometimes I wish I could die
That's a lie
I always want to die
But I can't, not yet
There isn't enough pain inside
I cry

I Fight

I fight the tears

I don't want to wash away the pain

I want it to sit and smolder

Like a fire with no more fuel

I fight death

Refusing to let it swallow me once again

I want to win, not lose

But I've lost so much already

I prayed for the baby, too late

The damage was done

I can't release the blame

It was my fault

I fight the hate that builds

Trying to find the love

It is hidden from me

Hidden well

I fight life

Like I never did before

But it remains the same

Filled with pain

I fight myself

I'm losing

I'm winning

Slowly, very slowly, I'm dying

I Love Two Weeks of You

We've begun
Taken slowly
Scared of what lies there
Walking blindfolded
Through an invisible maze
Thinking clearly
Lessened rage
Pushing forward
Parting the pain
Falling behind
Losing time
Coasting along
A comfortable pace
Doubts and uncertainties
That have no place
The feelings changing
Growing slow
Since I want to stay
Is it time to go?
I will not live in fear
I will love
In enlightenment

I See Said The Blind Man

It collapses upon itself

I see the hole

The opening

But it's too fast

I can't release

Because it's releasing me

I catch the points of ecstasy

I feel them

But I don't know where they are

I look for the points of ecstasy

But I can't see them

I can only see them when I can't

They close too fast

They're there but I can't tell you where

They are there

When I look back I see them

When I look ahead I see the ones to come

But when I look at them

They close too fast

I see nothing

But I see everything at once

I see said the blind man

Misconception

Smoke curls blue from his lips, as he sits and ponders what's next

What demon's dream will show itself, to the eye inside his mind

Offer up your sacrifice, he takes it without pause

The day slowly fades into night, as life fades into death

Amazing as he plows on through, everything you have

Standing with his palms outstretched, bring me more he said

A golden boy walks in the room, hiding what's in his hand

You have not tried this my friend, I think it will be your end

He smiles slightly as it's handed to him, he throws it down his mouth

Laughter raises from his lips, his pupils slip in and out

Silence falls over the room, the world holding it's breath

He dreams of when his life would be, nothing but the best

When he returns from the other place, a place we have not been

A smile barely escapes his lips, as he ponders once again

Am I God he often thinks, as the buzz hits him in waves

Am I God he often thinks, will I put you in your graves

Smoke curls blue from his lips, as he sits and ponders what's next

What demon's dream will show itself, to the eye inside his mind

Offer up your sacrifice, he takes it without a pause

The day slowly fades into night, as life fades into death

<u>My Love</u>

The turns and toils of making love
Everyday conversation is something more
The past can not die with pain in one's eyes
Asking why, why did I lie
I lied to save, save pain in the truth
Although you don't know, it did
Your anger will pass, the pain goes away
Waiting it out, the price I must pay
I remain with love in heart and wait
Wait for your mind to re-spool
I do understand, I always have
But can you understand me
I had no love, all was dead
Or so it was what you told me
I was alone and mad, I hated my life
Wanted you to be mine, be my wife
When you said no, it was all I could do
Not to die
So I made a mistake, I wanted revenge
I hurt myself instead
I love you so much, which will always be true
I'll never love anyone, anyone but you

Trials & Tribulations

Life's little trials

Trials and tribulations

Larger than they appear

The biggest problems

The end of the world

Fall short when sought to compare

Why can't it be easy?

Why can't it make sense?

Why must it always be hard?

Love is love

Or so it should be

Perhaps deep down it is

I wish I could have her

To love and to hold

I know I would never let go

I wish we could marry

Find us a home

Have children to make us so weary

I miss her so much

But this I can't say

Trying to save her the trouble

All the pain

I've ever felt

This has caused me double

<u>Set Her Free</u>

I awoke to the sound of cold rain striking the window
At once sadness consumes me to control my day
My love is complicated so that I can't understand
My heart lies broken, seems it's all I can say
No fault of hers, no fault of mine
The only fault can be laid upon time
Things changed too fast, life moves too slow
A guilty heart that's committed no crime
I love her so, with all of my heart
No matter how hard I try, I can't forget
She needs her time, time to heal
I know our love hasn't died, not yet
I've gone through too much pain and sorrow
I've fought too long for happiness to come
I want to do the right thing
To try and give her freedom
I still want to be with her
Be a part of her life always
I could never stop loving her
Love her the rest of my days
I could never live without her
She means the world to me
But if I'll ever have her
I must set her free

Sweet Surrender

Someone tore my heart out

Ripped it from my chest

Threw it to the ground

And laughed as he spit upon it

Proceeded to urinate on it

Kick it

Laughing all the time

Just as my heart

Lying there

Bleeding

Sweating

Pulsating

Coated with dirt and shards of glass

Looked as if it had died

One final beat

As if the angels sang

Our Heaven's light shone upon the Earth

He brought down the heel of his boot

Crushing my heart

Chunks of what was

Now lying still

I stand there

A gaping hole in my chest

As I fall to my knees

A summer breeze catches my soul

Carrying it from my shell

There my body will lay

With it all my pain

My Child

My heart beats sadness
While my child's could never beat
No fingers, no toes, no eyes to look up at me
But a soul? Yes. A soul very much his own
She asked me, can a child never born have a soul
Yes, for a thing with no soul, could cause no pain
My child, who never saw the Sun
My child, who never sang a song
My child, who never smelled the spring
My child, who never rode a swing
My child, who never shed a tear
My child, who never knew fear
My child, who never offered a smile
My child, who never walked a mile
My child, who never heard me speak
My child, who never got a peek
My child, who never loved another
My child, who never saw his mother
My child, who never lived a day
My child, who never heard me say
I love you

A World of Beauty

Once again the time is approaching

Time for me to leave the only home I've ever known

I'm confident I will one day return

Hopefully this time on my own terms

I watched the sky tonight

My eyes have steadily wandered to the sky of late

I watched as the Sun slowly set down to bed

A glowing orb just out of sight in the West

It seemed as though all was still, motionless

As if Michelangelo's brush stroked the clouds overhead

A beautiful pink in the East

Melting into a rich, dark red in the West

It filled me with the urge to cry

All has changed so fast in the short past

Friends have come who are now gone

This is where my thoughts lie, with their souls

I've done many things undeserving of their love

Yet I feel it still, I suppose I always will

It seems strange to me to find beauty still

A world that seems so cruel and evil

Reminding me of the truth that lies within

It is not this world that has caused me so much pain

But what the men placed upon it have done

The world will always be a beautiful place

And I must try not to make it uglier

As The Smoke

As the smoke clears
I see a picture
A man of ninety-one
Sitting naked at a desk
Listening to Beethoven
Writing a poem
As the smoke clears
I see a picture
A man of nineteen
Sitting naked at a desk
Listening to Beethoven
Writing a poem
As the smoke thickens
I see them clearly as one
A man
Sitting naked at a desk
Listening to Beethoven
Writing a poem
As the smoke clears
I see an empty chair
Sitting at a desk
Memories of Beethoven
And a poem

<u>We've Died</u>

When the Full Moon and Orion

Are joined in the sky

And the gates of Heaven

Stand before my eyes

I look over my shoulder

A glance behind

I've died

I step forward onto the cloud

But I'm too heavy

I'm falling through

Racing to the ground

With astonishing speed

Help me please

Someone catch me

Smack, I hit the Earth

But still I haven't stopped

Traveling through the world

I see civilizations dead and gone

I wonder where they went wrong

When I break through the other side

All life has ceased

The Sun and Orion

Are joined in the sky

And the gates of Heaven

Stand before my eyes

I look over my shoulder

A glance behind

We've died

<u>What Once Was</u>

Untouchable

Invincible

Immortal

Links of a chain

Slowly decaying

As links fall off

And float away

Weak

Desolate

Destroyed

Ancient ruins of what once was

Beauty to be forgotten

Leaving behind a mess

Sadness

Dismay

Sorrows

Cries for help

Calling out to the souls

Go unanswered

Goodbyes are pointless

Today is the last

Tomorrow shall not come

Remembrance

Forgiveness

Thankfulness

I hope I don't live long enough to see

You

Me

Us

Only what once was

The Coming Day

The night is my only friend that remains
It helps me, no it allows me to hide
I wish I could hide from all the pain
But wishes, I'm afraid don't come true
There's nothing true about true love
There's nothing I can do
Dreams only fill us with false hope
Life only waits to tear us down
Anything that I could ever want
Will never be something I'll ever hold
I must go on, go on alone
I try to take what I don't deserve
I want all the things I haven't earned
I'm sorry, I don't know what to do
If only you could be me, I could be you
I'll miss you no matter what may come
God what I wouldn't give to just be done
The night is my only friend that does remain
But all I can see is the coming day

Smokes

Veni Vidi Vici

Filter

20

Class A

Unlimited

Underage sale prohibited

Death in a box

Light up another

Miles and Miles

Warning of Generals

Women birthing low

In the surgeons hand

Flip-top U.S.A.

Father Philip

Mrs. Morris my neighbor

Death in a box

Light up another

Simple brown paper

Little white dots

60 black stripes

On paper so white

Marlboro man

Is a true friend

Death in a box

Light up another

Only A Poem

The horse is rocking
The chair has stopped
The Christmas lights shine bright
The fire burns so hot
The paint flakes off the ceiling
The house is filled with smoke
The presents lie underneath the tree
The children begin to choke
The dog lets out a yelp
The smoke alarm screams
The parents are out for the evening
The children are doomed it seems
The man who runs inside
Was sleeping in the cold
He's pulling out the children
Ten and nine years old
He goes back for the dog
He dies inside the house
One second he's a hero
The next he's a louse
The children want their presents
Mom and Dad are still not home
Christmas will go on
This is only a poem

<u>Hannah</u>

Why do I destroy love?
How do I lose control?
I love you with all my heart
This I know is true
Why do I live off of pain?
Why did I have to hurt you?
The tears won't come
But I know they're there
I've ruined my chance
You were all that I had
If you're gone forever
I can never forgive
I took our lovely flower
And tore it all to shreds
I will never love another
You're the only one there is
I've gained hate instead of trust
For this I must pay
I'll be forever without you
But I'll love you every day
I will never forget you
I can't ask you to forgive
And I will keep on loving you
As long as I live

<u>For Me</u>

A beginning

To an end

The first poem

Of many to come

My fourth Bible

Nothing's been done

Still I push on

I have no choice

I have a gift

Not to use it

Would make it shit

To close my eyes

Live a normal life

Would be to deny

The blade of the knife

That's cutting my soul

To give me my pain

All I have

That keeps me sane

I will write of many things

Love, death, life

The same

But I must write

Must write

For me

Infinite Solitude

I'm destined to go on alone
No one to share my heart
If I should find a love
We're surely destined to part
I won't wallow in self-pity
I won't cry myself to sleep
I'll take what I've been given
The benefits I shall reap
It's true I may grow lonely
At times I may be sad
But I can always remember
The love that I once had
And if I should grow foolish
And think that love I'll find
The foolishness shall pass
Or I will lose my mind
There is no woman for me
I will not find true love
Yet this does not control me
For I have risen above
Now I must forget this
And go on with my life
Never to be a father
Never to have a wife

<u>Valentine's Day</u>
The day of hearts
Lie broken in the street
A thirty story drop
As I look past my feet
A day of love for some
For others a day of sorrow
Twice I have failed
I refuse to see tomorrow
On this day of massacre
Spilled blood, bones and marrow
Cupid carefully strung his bow
He missed me with his arrow.
Even if he struck his mark
It really wouldn't matter
The only purpose it would serve
To make my heart grow sadder
A question what is love?
Goes without an answer
I was born my heart was broken
There's no cure for this cancer
I have lived my life so far
With a heart that isn't whole
I pray that this division
Isn't in my soul
Love must be destroyed
Destruction must be loved
From the roof of this building
I will fly like a dove

When my body hits the ground
Dead my soul won't be
The strangers will crowd around
The shell of me to see.

The Openings

I'm floating from my body
Flying through the air
Caught in ecstasy
Laughing without fear
All my worldly possessions
I have left behind
My heart, my soul, finally
Have become at one with my mind
Everyone I left there
Have all begun to cry
I hope they are aware
That I have learned to fly
In death I have found something
In life I never had
Love, peace, and happiness
No reason for you to be sad
I can finally sleep now
No need for me too breathe
All my pain is gone now
That's why I chose to leave
I can see the love now
The love that was always there
When it's time for you to join
You need not go in fear
I couldn't find the openings
Now that's all I see
No longer are they closing
Only waiting there for me

Standing In the cold

When is the time

That I will die

Should I prepare to go

I believe

That I am next

Tell me do you know

All the times you stopped me

Said I had to stay for you

And just like that you left me

Now I'm all alone

We grew so close together

I have to ask why

Was it so there'd be more pain

When it was time for you to die

I've always known life hates me

I never questioned why

Have I seen enough

Now can I please die

What the hell's my purpose

Why must I go on

Why do I deserve this

What did I do wrong

I'm supposed to take God

And put him in my heart

Just to make it easier

For Him to tear it apart

We could have gone together

You didn't have to go alone

You left me behind to rot here

Standing in the cold

<u>Run With Me</u>
Endless days
Turn to endless nights
When will it cease?
What you think is right
I think is wrong
When will there be peace?
Run with me
For the rest of time
We shall not be caught
Run with me
Don't fall behind
To everything we've fought
It's time to go
It's time to fly
We can not remain
There is no point
To fight the world
And swallow all the pain
Come let's go
Follow me
And we shall be released
For if we stay
Don't run away
The evil will never cease

Run with me
Run with me
As fast as we can go
Run with me
Run with me
Defeat we'll never know

?

When is it right to step in?

When is it right to back off?

When is it right to support?

When is it right to scoff?

Do we ever know what is right?

Do we ever know what is wrong?

I suppose we just have to wait

What if we wait too long?

Is it right to stand by your friends?

Even though you do not agree

Is it right to leave their side?

Is it right to let them be?

What if I know what is right?

When it's wrong for me to say

What if I am wrong?

What price will I have to pay?

What if I speak selfishly?

I think of only me

What if I hold it in?

Will I ever set it free?

What if I never say a word?

In the end I lose

What if I speak my heart?

What if I'm forced to choose?

Am I strong enough?

Can I accept whatever comes?

Will I break down and cry?

Have all my tears been used?

What if it doesn't matter?
It makes no difference at all
If I decide to stand
Eventually I will fall

<u>None Left</u>

My mind flows

Water from a glass

Petals of a rose

Lonely men pass

My hand begins to hurt

My eyes begin to tear

A beautiful young girl flirts

I will never get there

A gentle breeze blows

Snow falls to the ground

A seed begins to grow

I'm slowly falling down

A quest has begun

The search for nothing remains

My pants have come undone

My shoes are on the train

The sun still does shine

Even through the rain

I remember the taste of wine

It tastes just like champagne

The ashtrays are all full

The glasses stand unfilled

My arms refuse to pull

My mind is too strong-willed

My ties have all been cut

My hair falls one by one

The place I used to strut

Now my time is done

The pain is now forgotten
It was slowly all used up
Now I am left empty
The bottom of a cup

Leaving Home

The time is quickly approaching
The day that I shall leave
I'll miss my home intensely
But I'll return one day, you'll see
I'll go with a heart of sadness
Yet I have no other choice
It's true my friends I shall miss
But my fears I can not voice
For I must remain strong
And accept that which comes
I may be gone for very long
And lose the love of some
But I know in my heart
That my best friends will not leave
For if we are meant to part
This I can not believe
I love you all so truly
And this is how I know
The world may treat us cruelly
But we will not let go
So please do not forget me
Don't think I'm leaving you behind
Trust me and you will see
You'll always be in my mind
The time is quickly approaching
The day that I shall leave
I'll miss my home intensely
But I'll return one day, you'll see

<u>A Fathers Love</u>

One year is done

Another's begun

It's time to start again

Sleep now my child

The world's too wild

Everything is a sin

To shield you may be wrong

But I have heard the song

That the angels sing

The world is filled with hate

It's every man's true fate

That sadness death shall bring

I loved you from the start

With every piece of my heart

I will not let you go

There's so much to learn

Each day's slow burn

Too painful for you to know

Many years from now

You will learn how

Life is filled with pain

Yet every day you stay

The bad times burn away

The good ones all remain

<u>A True Test</u>

The day I knew was coming, has arrived
The decision has finally been made, I only sighed
Even though it didn't work I know, I tried
Finally now that I've decided to live, I haven't died
My future is ahead of me, my past is who I am
I can cure whatever ails me, no door has been slammed
The love has survived, through what is said no love can
Any man can love those that have died, I am more than man
I am a beautiful spirit, a soul that can shine on
I still feel love inside of me, I know what it's based upon
I am a being of love, a man that knows no ends
Whether I give to my love, or I give to my friends
A stranger is worth it, an enemy divine
I can give love, to anyone I find
I've wasted myself, up until this point in time
That will stop now, committed a horrible crime
I am everything, all that exists
It's in each one of us, the way it is
We each hold the secret, greatest secret of all
But if we never try, we'll never fall
If we never fall, we will never learn
The wheels of pain, will continue to turn
Don't be afraid, embrace what will come
I refuse to die, for the pleasure of some

<u>As Death Holds My Hand</u>

Pits of fire

In the heart of darkness

Yet they shed no light

A growing chill

A dark, damp feel

Adding to my fright

Shakily I move on

Slowly descending down

Into the darkest night of nights

The lizard sends out death calls

The snakes all call my name

It's time for me to die

Above is the Earth

With it's bright, warm sun

But that is all a lie

I am on my way

Won't see another day

No point to question why

There is no beauty here

It's never felt her touch

Going to the only place I can

I may have started out

A sweet and gentle child

But I'm an evil man

I receive what I deserve

Everlasting pain

As death holds my hand

Believe

I sit quietly listening, listening for my heart to break
My love's sweet smile is missing, it's all that I can take
I wish I could fly home, fly home into her arms
Then my pain could die, could cause me no more harm
I picture kissing her softly, looking in her eyes
I'm tired of all the sadness, all the tear-filled sighs
The Sun rises every morning, it sets at every night
Without her by my side, none of it seems right
I look up to the moon, I know she sees it too
I want to go be with her, there's nothing I can do
I light another cigarette, to forget about my pain
Sitting here without her, I feel I'll go insane
She calls to say she loves me, I hear it in her voice
The pain she's feeling also, I say I had no choice
For us to be together, we have to be apart
For happiness in the future, I now must break my heart
When again I finally see her, how will I bring myself to leave
One day we'll be back together, that's what we have to believe
There will be those that try to stop us, those that stand in our way
Our love for each other is true, that's all that we can say
If they don't understand this, say that it's not true
You'll look at me with love in your eyes, and I will look at you
To them we will smile quickly, then be upon our way
For we only need each other, love growing stronger day by day

Crazy

This place is getting crazy
Perhaps it's always been
If I don't get out soon
It's going to suck me in
My God this place is crazy
Everyone's gone nuts
To think I used to love it here
Now I don't know what
Has it always been this crazy?
Did I just figure it out?
Am I one of the crazies?
I just want to scream and shout
Are you all fucking crazy?
Can't any of you see?
Or is it completely normal?
Could it just be me?
Do you think it's crazy?
Does anyone agree?
Could it all be in my mind?
No it couldn't be
This place must be getting crazy
Or have I just been blind?
Have I lost my sanity?
It's so damned hard to find
Am I doing the right thing?
Is it right for me to leave?
If I stay here any longer
I'll go crazy I believe

Thank God I have my thoughts
They will keep me sane
Or perhaps they'll drive me crazy
When they're all that does remain

My King Has Fallen

My hair is getting longer
My mind's beginning to change
My hurt is getting stronger
This feeling I have is strange
I'm thinking a little more clearly
In between my alcoholic daze
My legs are growing weary
My eyes are getting crazed
My stomach's getting smaller
My words come out deranged
My writing's getting better
No longer do I feel caged
My life is getting easier
It's getting harder too
My woman are getting sleazier
My world is turning blue
My highs are getting deeper
Depression pulls me down
My smiles are getting brighter
As they turn into a frown
Spring is coming near
The leaves are turning brown
I must have missed the summer
I must have been coming down
I'm beginning to fly much higher
Before falling to the ground
My body begins to tire
When there's excitement all around

The nights are growing darker
Just before the dawn
I'm afraid my King has fallen
Taken by a lowly pawn

<u>The Golden Line</u>

Jealous fits of rage
Intertwined with squeals of delight
For those who love the sun
Those who embrace the night
If only sleep wasn't needed
If it wasn't loved so much
If my love wasn't breathing
If the truth wasn't such
Tears of failed endeavors
Screams of total pain
If the world wasn't so damn evil
If sorrow wasn't rain
Questions with no answers
Answers open more
If what was right was right
If Lady Luck wasn't such a whore
If someone wasn't tugging
On the strings that tie my mind
If your brother is your enemy
If the enemy is kind
Wars will be forgotten
Only time can tell
If life was simply easy
If we didn't make it hell
If what was wrong was wrong
If what was true was true
Then I will gladly be wrong
For what's a man to do?

Something

I've tried to die
It wouldn't take
I've tried to live
It was all so fake
Just sittin' around
Waitin' for something
Something to take me away
I've pursued my dreams
Watched them fade
I lost all hope
Progress I made
Just sittin' around
Waiting for something
Something to take me away
I left my home
I returned
I stuck with my roots
My tree house burned
Just sittin' around
Waiting for something
Something to take me away
I found my love
I threw it away
I settled for loneliness
Togetherness came
Just sittin' around
Waiting for something
Something to make me stay

Strength, Serenity, and Peace of Mind

I hold here in my hand
Strength, serenity, and peace of mind
All you have to do is take it
The answers you shall find
These things are what you need
To help you on your way
Take them from my hand
From your path you will not stray
I offer you this gift
It's all that I can give
The first is so important
It's the strength to live
Serenity is the second
It will allow you to be kind
After you possess these two
You'll then have peace of mind
I know that you can't see it
You don't think that it exists
Please, for me, receive it
The pain will not persist
I recently have found these
For my journey I will use
I'd like to share them with you
Now it's time to choose
Can you put your faith inside me?
I'm asking for your trust
Take these things from my hand
Pretend for me if you must

Take these from my hand
You they shall protect
Strength, serenity, and peace of mind
They're all that I have left

Religion

Is time the true factor?

Or is it really love?

Is pain the final answer?

Are any of these the one?

What is the meaning of life?

This question has no point

For if we knew the answer

Would we still decide to join?

Or would we all give up?

Would life come to an end?

Does it really matter?

Is death our only friend?

I for one won't worry

I refuse to buckle in

If I think that life is bullshit

Do you think that is a sin?

Why work only to get nowhere?

If you could only show me proof

You put all your faith in religion

And you stand there all aloof

What if you're living a lie?

You just don't know the truth

Is religion just big business?

Are they taking you all for fools?

Perhaps the pope is laughing

As the money comes rolling in

Perhaps you've just been taken

The greatest con there's ever been

I fear not eternal damnation
How bad could it be?
If I'm destined to meet Satan
The I'll just wait and see

Give Me What I Need

Voices speak softly so as not to be heard
Messages passed upon wings of the bird
The bird is a vulture, feeding on our souls
Those that give him his power don't know
They speak without thinking, care not who they harm
Realization of how short is my arm
Battles play over and again in my mind
Fights I can't fight, enemies I can't find
I longed for help with this loneliness I possess
I received depression, a fucked up mess
I love my baby, this will always be true
The peace that I needed I wanted from you
What you gave, was frustration and hate
You tried to make it all better too late
Now there's another to add to my list
A list of people I will never miss
One I used to care for and consider a friend
Now will mean nothing to me in the end
Oh well, that's life, who needs them anyway
I guess I have nothing left to say
Please next time when I call in need
Try not to add more to make my heart bleed
Just tell me you love me and always will
So I can tell you I miss you, and love you still

Don't Be Afraid, Set Him Free

People see their loved ones and it causes fear
No one wants to believe they were really there
It scares them to see what they don't understand
Unable to reach out and take their hand
The love that was, never dies
You'll see the love, look in his eyes
There's no need to be afraid
He won't hurt you in any way
Everyone takes comfort knowing he's here
Yet still they grow afraid to see him there
He's come to make it known he still loves
He's come to show us all that he's not gone
He stands to tell you it will be alright
Your screams and tears make him hide in the night
Remember the love, hold out your hand
Bring him in your heart, stand where he stands
Listen to his words that flow from his heart
He doesn't want the sadness to tear you apart
He loves you now, as he always did
Loved as a man, loved as a kid
He's with you now, as he'll always be
He just wants you to live, to set him free

Footprints Without a Sound

Life is so confusing, with all it's twists and turns
It's blows can be so bruising, it's nectar always burns
Life is extremely tiny, as it envelops all around
It's meaning slips right by me, leaving footprints without a sound
Life can be so brutal, so cold and incredibly cruel
To fight it seems so futile, accept it is the rule
Life can be imprisonment, while not allowing you to live
Happiness must be heaven sent, which only God can give
Tears may flow on endlessly, they can't stop the pain
Sorrow can swallow any man, driving him insane
Love is not forever, sometimes it must die
All ties can not be severed, for love you must always try
Nothing is without something, something never was
Joy is spread by laughing, bringing a gentle buzz
Friends will last forever, even after they die
And those who are most clever, still ask the question why
Living is for the wise, death is for the great
If we close our eyes, we may open them too late
I wish I understood it, I wish it all made sense
If I could only control it, if the problems weren't so dense
Life is so confusing, with all it's twists and turns
It's blows can be so bruising, it's nectar always burns
Life is extremely tiny, as it envelops all around
It's meaning slips right by me, leaving footprints without a sound

<u>I Shall Not Be Missed</u>

Cinnamon tulips

And sugartree buds

My this world is sweet

Desperate starvation

And killing fields

The world lies in defeat

Yellow stars

In a tangerine sky

Float upon true bliss

The answer hate

To the question why

What kind of world is this?

A comfortable numb

A gentle buzz

Contribute to content

Frightened of the future

Scared of what was

Tired of the present

Fly away

Softly fall

No worries to possess

The stench of death

Covers all

Mother Nature we slowly undress

No bodies here

Only souls

All that do exist

No loving here

Only fear

And I shall not be missed

<u>Inside the Lines</u>

One more chance

To make things right

One more chance

To bring the light

One more chance

To end the night

One more chance

To draw inside the lines

One more day

To prove to you

All the things I've wanted to

To treat you like

A queen to be

Cause that is all you'll ever be

To me

One more chance

To make things right

One more chance

To bring the light

One more chance

To end the night

One more chance

To draw inside the lines

Unconditional

Do you wonder

What the future holds?

I believe I know

Do you question

Why you're here?

You should have no fear

There's coming a time

When we must choose

Collectively as one

Do we put our faith

In Satan's hands

Or the almighty God and his son?

Most will choose unknowingly

To follow the prince of evil

This will inevitably

Lay death upon your table

I will choose in good faith

To stand beside the latter

And when I die, I will know

Nothing else will matter

Jesus Christ stands by my side

I know he always will

And if on my path I should fall

I know He'll love me still

The Sun Will Shine Again One Day

No matter how dark and dismal the sky should grow

The sun will shine again one day

No matter where you are, or where you go

The sun will shine again one day

Look past the darkness cold and grey

The sun will shine again one day

Stay on your path, never stray

The sun will shine again one day

Don't be afraid, don't run away

The sun will shine again one day

Don't listen to the words they say

The sun will shine again one day

Stand strong, never fall

The sun will shine again one day

If you can not walk, then you must crawl

The sun will shine again one day

Keep me in mind, I'll be on your side

The sun will shine again one day

No need to cry, don't try to hide

The sun will shine again one day

I'll be there with the sun's soft rays

The sun will shine again one day

Out of the west, like a gentle breeze

The sun will shine again one day

Spider

A spider in the corner of my room
The flowers in the vase are out of bloom
The walls are filled with medals that are not mine
And the man inside my clothes is out of line
The question in my mind is but the same
The ghosts outside my window call my name
The trees outside do shutter with no breeze
Now I must take roll on who believes
Those who do not can not follow me
And those who do shall be the ones set free
A pebble of pain that drives deep inside my mind
The cure for this is something I won't find
The past is in the future once again
How can we define what's never been?
The end of the beginning has yet to come
But the beginning of the end has begun for some
The flame that lights my death is not the same
The future of the present never came
The ties between my mind have come undone
The bricks have walled me in behind the sun
My world has turned itself all upside down
And the end is sure to come without a sound
A spider in the corner of my room
And still he has decided not to move

Summer Sunrise

Who's to say which way the wind blows
Who's to say where the shadows throw
When does the sun reach the other side
When is it time to run and hide
Why is it cold in the winter time
Why is the summer so fine
On a summer morning
The air's so crisp
The clear blue sky
As the day begins
On a summer morning
When the sun does rise
A beautiful sight
To unworthy men's eyes
The last of the miracles
For this world to see
Looked upon
Ungratefully
But there's always those
Who can realize
The beauty there
As the sun does rise
And with a heart
Filled with love
Give thanks for this miracle
Sent from above

<u>Crushed Again</u>

What I want is impossible
What I need isn't there
I think of her eyes
Her beautiful hair
I think of what was
What will never be
The man behind the smile
Will never be me
Life throws a twist
Where one shouldn't be
One more love locked
I don't have the key
Every time I love
All I do is lose
I may deserve love
But whose?
Do I deserve it at all?
Or is this just a lie?
Do I need the pain
Simply to get by?
It's easier not to care
It's easy to give in
So why can't I do it?
How cruel this life has been
And I have paid it back
With cruelty in return
Please just let me go
I'm tired of the burn

We're always chasing happiness
And this we can not find
Just when I think I've found it
It can not be mine
I'm sorry for my past sins
For all the things I've done
My soul's been burning candles
I'm on my final one
As I watch the wax drip down
The wick slowly burn away
I live the rest of my life
Waiting for the day
And when the wax has melted
The flame dwindled away
I'll look up to the heavens
Thank you I will say

<u>I Have Paid My Dues</u>
The words slowly fade into the page
It's as if they've always been
These words aren't set in stone
Just scratches of a pen
The days slowly fade into life
How perfectly they fit
The good next to the bad
They all sum up to shit
My loves fade into past
Along with them my friends
We wasted all that time
Waiting for the end
Well the end never came
And now it's time to go
It's strange that as I get older
The easier the words flow
I realize I'm on my own
No one here can save me
All the love we had
Where did we get really?
We truly thought we were special
It was so easy to believe
I must find why I'm special
That's why I must now leave
It's true that I still love them
I most likely always will
I feel like I've been waiting
And I'm waiting still

I believe our time's been wasted
This may not be true
But I must walk away
For I have paid my dues

Meant to Be

As I turn the pages
The words continue to flow
Now will live forever
What wasn't a moment ago
Why do I have this power
This I'll never know
But I promise I shall use it
Until the day I go
I do not control it
Although it comes from me
I'd be stupid to think I own it
It was simply meant to be
If I knew who I should thank
For this ability I've received
I could not find a way
To repay him equally
So all that I can do
Is use it all my days
And write so many words
So many different ways
Until I reach perfection
With a contented sigh
I'll gladly close my eyes
And then I shall die

Second Messiah

Man is destined

To burn out

Destroying ourselves

On a daily basis

An explosion

Impending

The day we all shall die

The second messiah

A reigning king

Will take the children

And make them sing

Man will be judged

By God's hand

Find his love

It's never too soon

If you wait

Wait too long

Your gentle heart

Will miss the song

Satan will be

Defeated in the end

God won't turn his back

If you love him my friend

We will see

The end of the world

With it a beginning

Listen to the word

Open your heart
Let the Lord in
He will forgive
No matter what your sin

Joey

I see you there
Floating in the sky
Smiling down at me
You've learned to fly
We're all here
To say good-bye
The question returns
The question why
You're growing more distant
As you fly away
I wish I could stop you
Tell you to stay
You know we love you
Always will
We know you loved us
You'll love us still
I'm going to miss you
With all of my heart
I never thought it'd come
The day we would part
I love you my brother
Love 'til the end
It won't be over
'Til we're there again
Good-bye my friend
Fly away
I don't know how much longer
I can stay

<u>Conform</u>

Turn the coffee on

Make sure you flip those eggs

Please don't burn the toast

Now you've ruined my day

What will you do with your life?

Will you find a job today?

If you think you'll get by without school

There is no possible way

It's so important now

It means the rest of your life

Don't you want to have kids?

Well, you'll never find a wife

If you think you'll just get by

Well, you're living out a dream

Do you think that life's a game?

Well, it's not as easy as it seems

Do you think we give out free rides?

Don't you have a plan?

If you keep living like a child

You'll never be a man

Don't let it pass you by

Use the brain you have

You need to join society

You need a swift kick in the ass

You can always write

Become something first

You need something to fall back on

If worst comes to worst

I don't want to fall back
I won't give up my dream
Maybe if you had one
You might know what I mean

<u>Faith?</u>

Days have come and gone
Memories slowly fade
The pain is ever strong
For the mistakes we all made
Guilt fills my mind
Can't make it go away
When will it be my time
I know I can not stay
How can I go on
When I pray to die
Something's very wrong
Why should I have to try
I long to be with you
Until the end of time
I know my love is true
Is that such a crime
Won't you take me away
From this evil place
Does it help to pray
Is faith just a waste
I was forced to live
Many years ago
No mercy did you give
Now pain is all I know
Thank you for the love
That my heart you gave
With one act from above
You took it all away

The Little Elves

I've danced with the little elves
And listened to their songs
They've told me all their stories
They've been here all along
Most humans never see them
Or know that they exist
But they have picked up everything
That we have ever missed
They live in a world of fantasy
In a state of total bliss
They can destroy your problems
With a simple little kiss
When you lose your favorite sock
Or your earrings while you sleep
You can be sure that they have found them
And these things they shall keep
Until the day you need them most
When you think that you might die
They shall put them where you'll find them
With a twinkle in their eye
They live to cause mischief
Drive you crazy 'til the end
But when you truly need them
They shall always be your friend
I've danced with the little elves
And listened to their songs
They've told me all their stories
They'll be here all along

<u>At Every Morning's Dawn</u>
You've worked so hard
To get where you are
You deserve the best
I look in your eyes
And with little surprise
I find you're better than the rest
Now it's time
For you to push on
To bigger and better things
Leave the past behind
Expand your mind
Spread apart your wings
No longer do you need
What began with just a seed
And grew into your home
Nothing to hold you down
Rise up from the ground
The world is yours to roam
But one day you'll return
To the place that you first learned
Nothing is stronger than love
And the loved ones from the past
Will gather around at last
And rise in the flight of the dove
We'll miss you while you're gone
And at every morning's dawn
We shall think of you
And as we wait for your return
A candle we will burn
Our love forever true

Conversation on the Other Side

How are you son?

My trip? Long

Have your uncles been taking care of you?

I knew they would

Where are they anyway?

I thought they'd be here to meet me

That's good, I've waited so long to see them

Will you take me there?

Good, let's hurry

I guess you're right

We do have all the time in the world

I'm sorry for what I did to you

Of course you know

Your mother's fine

But I don't think she'll be here for some time

Is this it?

It's beautiful

Aren't you coming in?

You're right, I suppose we should be alone

My God, It's good to see you guys again

I missed you so much

Everyone misses you

I'm sorry it took me so long to keep the pact, but it was a big decision

I can't believe how amazing it is here

Come on, let's pull a few and I'll tell you everything

By the way, who do you think will be coming next?

The Hall of Light

I've been walking down a hall now for eighteen years. As I've walked I've
closed hundreds of doors behind me. I decide to stop and look at how far
I've come. I turn to see six shafts of light from the sides and a strangely
glowing doorway in front of me. The doorway is where I entered the hall.
The six shafts of light are the doors I have opened and the rooms I have
entered. When inside I soaked in the feelings of ecstasy and carried
them in my heart as I continued my journey. The first shaft of light
throws silhouettes of the friends I made as a child. The remaining five
each have a silhouette of their own. Even from this distance I can make
out the shadows of my brothers. Once again I look ahead to the end of
the hall. Here I see another doorway with that same strange glow. It
seems so far away that it may take fifty years to reach. The hallway is
long and as black as night. This blackness fills me with a feeling of fear
and sorrow, but it's impossible to go back. I stand there for some time,
confused as to what I should do. I'm torn between wishing I could go
back and praying that the end wouldn't be so far. Finally, I look to one
side and push open a door. I step into the room and allow the light, the
feeling of ecstasy, soak into my deprived body. My memory didn't serve
justice to the feeling that filled me. After I had bathed completely in the
light I once again stepped out into the hall. I look behind me and find
with great sorrow that the lights have grown more distant. Yet, when I
turn, I find to my surprise that the end grows nearer. Not only that, but
there are several mere cracks of light, doors waiting to be opened.
Eventually, I open the last door, soak in the final light, and stand at the
threshold of the second glowing doorway. There is no door here, only the
doorway and that oddly brilliant, beckoning light. There is no escape,
and no choice to be made. I take one final gaze down the long hallway
now brilliantly lit with shafts of light from opened doors, all of them
throwing silhouettes of love from the long journey. There are a few dark
spots of doors never opened, but not many. My body is suddenly filled

with that feeling of ecstasy. This is the first time I've felt this in the hallway and it feels wonderful. Along with the ecstasy comes a sense of accomplishment and pride. I turn to the doorway filled with confidence, prepared to accept whatever I may find inside. As I step into the room, I step into bliss. I'm surrounded by all of the experiences I found in all of those light filled rooms, behind the open doors. This is my reward for walking that long hall, and opening those millions of doors when it would have been so easy to give up. Here I will gladly spend eternity.

That Which Is True

Love is all powerful, all we really need
In our quest to find it, we must love all that we see
Love is understanding, both the good and the bad
It is finding your soul, stop making it sad
Our soul is who we are, invisible as life
Shown in only secrets, bits and pieces flying by
Our souls long for love, to give and to receive
To share our love with others, help them to believe
Our bodies do constrict us, our minds cloud what is right
They hide what's truly in us, keep our beauty out of sight
Love is all important, knowledge is the key
For I can learn from you, in turn you learn from me
Knowledge is understanding, both the good and the bad
Finding love inside ourselves, the loves our souls have had
Learning is a life-long process, not to be smart but to be wise
To find love within everyone, see it hidden in their eyes
I strive for understanding, can never possess enough
I can never stop searching, to understand out of love
Man has become too hateful, an absence of the light
Hiding in the shadows, keeping themselves out of sight
I wish that I could help them, make them understand
This is but a small part of existence, temporarily a man
Life is understanding, both the good and the bad
Life is love and knowledge, death is far from sad